骨骼攻击

GUGE GONGJI

骨骼
攻击

Master Hei Long

GUGE GONGJI

Seven Primary Targets to Take Anyone Out of a Fight

PALADIN PRESS
BOULDER, COLORADO

Also by Master Hei Long:

Danger Zones: Defending Yourself against Surprise Attack

Dragons Touch: Weaknesses of the Human Anatomy

Iron Hand of the Dragon's Touch: Secrets of Breaking Power

Master's Death Touch: Unarmed Killing Techniques

Master's Guide to Basic Self-Defense: Progressive Retraining of the
    Reflexive Response

21 Techniques of Silent Killing

Guge Gongji:
Seven Primary Targets to Take Anyone Out of a Fight
by Master Hei Long

Copyright © 1991 by Master Hei Long

ISBN 0-87364-635-5
Printed in the United States of America

Published by Paladin Press, a division of
Paladin Enterprises, Inc., P.O. Box 1307,
Boulder, Colorado 80306, USA.
(303) 443-7250

Direct inquires and/or orders to the above address.

CONTENTS

INTRODUCTION

Generally, there are three ways to halt an incoming opponent:

1. You can beat him off with speed, power, and tactical strategy without going after major target areas.

2. You can disable or knock him out with attacks to the central nervous system (CNS) or peripheral nervous system (PNS).

3. You can neutralize his motion by damaging his anatomical framework, thereby rendering his body incapable of normal movement.

The first method has a lot to recommend it. It offers a multitude of options, lets the defender use techniques with which he is most familiar, and allows him to use reflex movement as opposed to a specified system of fighting that may be unnatural for his body type.

The second method should be used by snappy, sharpshooter-type fighters who can get inside an opponent's defenses quickly and safely, making accurate contact with smaller targets.

The third method, which is the focus of this book, is an intense, second-to-last resort. It should be used only when you face a larger, stronger opponent who is unwilling to negotiate a peaceful settlement to the dispute and is intent on doing serious harm to you—and when you do not want to inflict a lethal or permanently disabling injury on him.

I do not believe in taking a life unnecessarily, anymore than I believe in harming a person without cause to do so. But we cannot always choose the intensity with which we engage in personal combat. Consequently, there may come a time when you are forced to kill or be killed. In such a case, you must do what you have to do; you have no choice. However, in situations where you are not necessarily facing death but the odds against you are too great to take risks, you have an alternative. You can break—but not destroy—the instrument of danger.

To stop a speeding car, you don't have to injure the driver; you can blow the tires out. To stop a plane from taking off, you don't have to blow up the cockpit or kill the pilot; you can damage a wing.

By eliminating an opponent's physical ability to pursue and engage you, you eliminate the immediate threat he poses. It is highly unlikely that an opponent will throw a punch with an arm that has a broken wrist or elbow, and his ability to advance on you would be substantially inhibited by a broken knee or ankle. Structurally disabling an opponent compares with removing bullets from a gun. Both weapons, for the most part, are rendered harmless.

Guge gongji, meaning "attacking the structure," is that study in lian shi kung fu that focuses on damaging the limbs and the neck. Only one of the seven primary targets in this study is potentially lethal; the rest will simply deflate a tire or damage a wing, so to speak. This is not to say that these targets are minor ones. In fact, they are critical targets whose damage will have long-term consequences to an opponent and should be applied only when conventional defensive tactics are not likely to be effective.

CHAPTER ONE

The Biomechanics of Motion

Let's begin with an elementary examination of human body structure and movement. To get the most benefit from this book, you should understand the biomechanics of posture, motion, and the body's architecture. A knowledge of how cartilage, articulations (joints between cartilage or bone), and synovial fluid (the lubricating fluid secreted by articulations) affect muscular activity is helpful. Unlike early martial arts students, today we have the advantages of medical science and the opportunity to examine the findings of decades of analysis into the structure and function of the human body. Acquiring this knowledge will greatly enhance your perception of your body, as well as your opponent's, as both target and weapon.

The human skeleton is composed of 206 bones joined by either fibrous, cartilaginous, or synovial articulations, or joints. Fibrous articulations are immovable, such as those binding the various bones of the skull. Cartilaginous articulations are slightly movable, such as those connecting the vertebrae. Synovial articulations are free moving, such as those at the elbows and knees.

To appreciate fully the necessity of movable bone junctions, imagine for a moment that all of your 206 bones were solidly fused together. There would be no movement at your toes, ankles, knees, hips, fingers, wrists, elbows, shoulders, or spinal column. You would be unable to walk, raise your arms, turn your head, or even sit up and feed yourself. Without constant nursing to take care of your simplest needs, you would perish. Your muscles would atrophy, or waste away. Even breathing would be difficult. Without movement of the thorax, allowing for the flexion of the ribs, the expansion and contraction of the diaphragm would be constricted.

The proper functioning of each of our joints is necessary for even rudimentary bodily movements. Needless to say, the elimination of an opponent's control over the movements of his joints or the mobility governing those joints will substantially diminish his effectiveness.

The movement of bones follows the contraction or relaxation of corresponding muscles, which pull the bones in a desired direction. If the articulation of a pair of bones does not guide the affected structures along their designated course, there can be no control over the direction of the movement. Although adjoining bone surfaces have corresponding impressions or protrusions that allow their ends to attach to related bones, ligaments and joint capsules are needed to keep these surfaces in position. Without ligaments to tie bone endings together and help control their range of motion, any applied muscle force would pull the bones out of their sockets, neutralizing the intended effort. Obviously, muscles and bones are useless without solid, functional joints.

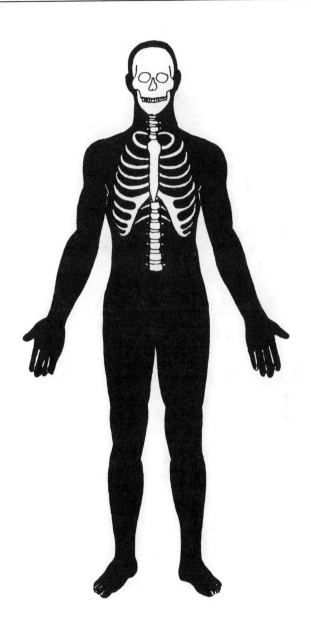

In anatomy, the skeleton is separated into two divisions: the axial skeleton and the appendicular skeleton.

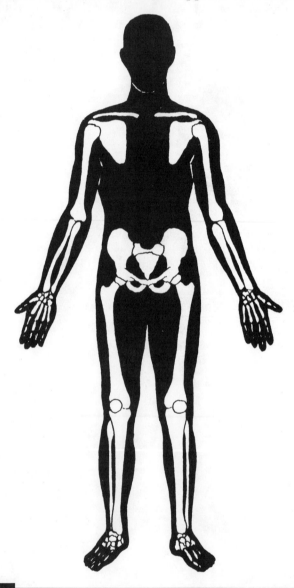

FIGURE 2   **Appendicular Skeleton**

The axial skeleton (Figure 1) is named for its central position in the body, providing points of attachment for the appendages and an axis to maintain posture. The primary function of the axial skeleton is to protect the vital organs. The skull protects the brain and sensory organs, and the vertebrae shield the spinal cord. The sternum and rib cage surround the cardiopulmonary organs and muscles that control the two most vital physiological functions: blood circulation and breathing.

The appendicular skeleton (Figure 2) consists of the hip and shoulder girdles, the clavicle, and the four limbs. This portion of the anatomy provides mobility and service to the axial skeleton. Without the appendages, the axial body would be unable to move about, care for, or protect itself.

The ability to control the body's locomotion is the key to our study. Up to this point we have stressed the necessity of properly functioning joints for performing the most basic tasks. We will now examine one such joint during movement.

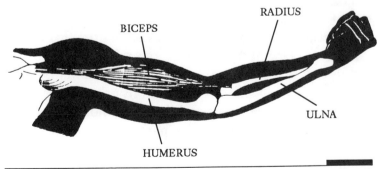

FIGURE 3

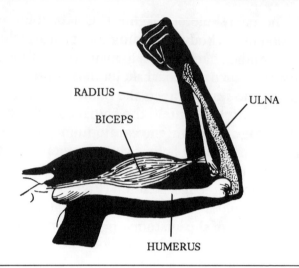

RADIUS
ULNA
BICEPS
HUMERUS

FIGURE 4

Observe Figures 3 and 4. Figure 3 depicts a left arm with a 35-degree bend. To maintain this position, static contraction of the biceps is necessary. Force is being applied to the radius where the biceps is inserted, and the articulation of the humerus, radius, and ulna is under pressure. When motion contraction is applied by the biceps, the distal end of the arm, or that farthest from the body, travels toward the shoulder as illustrated in Figure 4. Note that the ulna has maintained its position at the tip of the humerus. (The radius also joins with the humerus, but that juncture is not visible from this view.) This joint is formed by impressions in the ulna and the radius that ride on the rounded tip of the humerus. The humerus has two smooth depressions upon which they glide. The joint capsules and ligaments hold the radius and the ulna in their respective positions.

Now look at Figure 5. This illustration depicts what might happen to the two bones of the forearm if the ligaments maintaining their position at the tip of the humerus were broken. Note that the ulna (the shaded bone) has slipped off the distal tip of the humerus and traveled toward the proximal end. Because the ulnar and radial bones have slipped out of position on the humerus, the motion contraction of the biceps is unable to affect the flexion of the arm achieved in Figure 4.

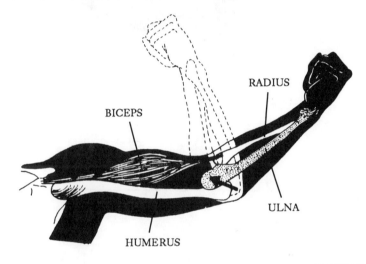

FIGURE 5

The smooth motion of joints is facilitated by the construction of a joint capsule. Observe Figure 6, which illustrates two common bones forming a joint. Note that the tips of the bones are covered by cartilage. Synovial fluid between the articular cartilages lubricates the cartilaginous tips. A synovial membrane encapsulates the articulating surfaces, and a fibrous capsule seals the junction. It is this complex construction of joints that permits them to move smoothly without grinding away the bones or sticking together like a rusted hinge.

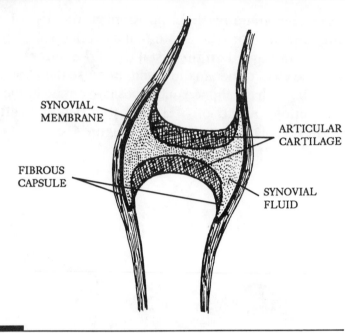

SYNOVIAL
MEMBRANE

ARTICULAR
CARTILAGE

FIBROUS
CAPSULE

SYNOVIAL
FLUID

FIGURE 6

The joint capsule and the ligaments that bind articulating surfaces together allow the muscular system to
affect movements of the skeletal system. Just as muscles
rely on the strength of their tendons to pull bones in a
desired direction, bones rely on firm ligaments to bind
their ends together. Only through strong, properly functioning joints is the muscular system able to exert force
over the skeleton to cause motion. A neutralized joint
inhibits the ability to move the related bones in a controlled effort. In this book, we will focus on specific
skeletal joints.

CHAPTER TWO

The Seven Primary Targets

You should now have a basic understanding of the human skeleton, how the bones are joined together, how muscles affect movement of the skeleton, and the crucial role of properly functioning joints. This understanding will allow you to visualize the effects brought about by damaging any one of the seven primary targets we are about to discuss.

Think of the body as a machine with many moving parts, all interrelated and necessary to its successful functioning. The enhanced illustration of the skeleton in Figure 7 clearly depicts the location, shape, and junction of the skeletal bones, seven of which are the primary targets we will focus upon.

Structurally, damaging a joint neutralizes all corresponding bones that attach to it. Neurologically, damaging a joint immobilizes it and the joints above and below it. Consequently, significant damage to any four of the following primary targets—elbow, knee, ankle, or wrist—puts the entire corresponding quarter of the body out of

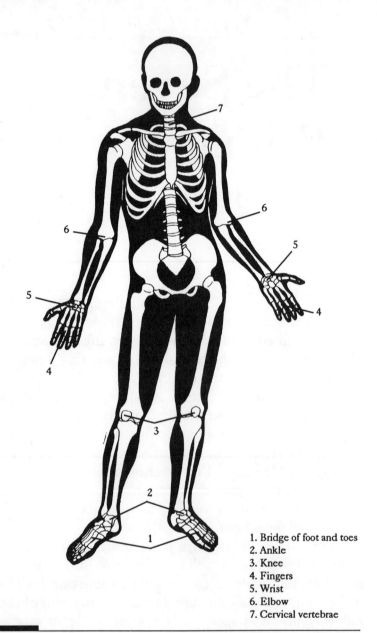

1. Bridge of foot and toes
2. Ankle
3. Knee
4. Fingers
5. Wrist
6. Elbow
7. Cervical vertebrae

FIGURE 7   **Seven Primary Targets**

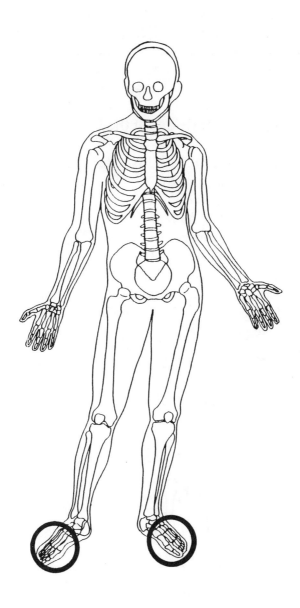

Target 1: Foot and Toes   *FIGURE 8*

commission. If the right elbow is damaged, the whole right arm is neutralized. Damaging a knee has similar consequences to the corresponding leg. The more near, or proximal, the target, the more extensive the results of the attack.

Target Number 1: Bridge of the Foot and Toes

Observe Figure 8. Your first target is the bridge of the foot (metatarsals) and the toes (metatarsal phalanges). Figure 9 shows an overhead view of the foot. As the illustration depicts, the metatarsals and the metatarsal phalanges are small, individual bones. They form the shape of the foot and allow for its flexion. The multifaceted structure of the foot and toes allows us to support our entire body weight as we walk. Damage to this area interrupts the body's ability to effectively transfer weight from one leg to the other.

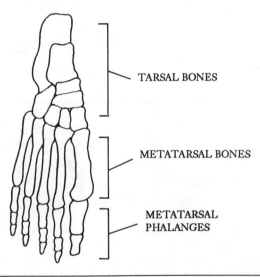

TARSAL BONES

METATARSAL BONES

METATARSAL PHALANGES

FIGURE 9   **Overhead View of Foot**

In Figure 10 an enhanced side view of the entire foot and ankle illustrates the metatarsals and their corresponding toes from the outside. Because the bridge and the ball of the foot are also used as weapons, damaging this target area incapacitates potential weapons as well as a supportive structure.

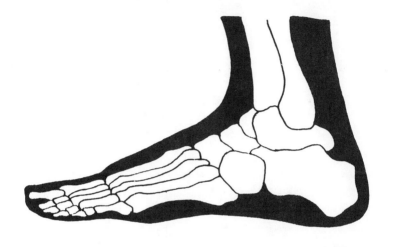

Foot and Ankle Joint   *FIGURE 10*

Target Number 2: Ankle

Observe Figure 11. Your second primary target is the ankle (tarsus). An ankle generally gives way when the foot is twisted laterally, often accidentally because of an improperly placed or supported step. The damage usually consists of a hyperextended ligament and/or compressed tarsal bones, causing minor damage to the cartilage. In most cases, the victim of such an injury immediately drops to the ground, either by choice to alleviate the pain or as a result of the nervous system responding to

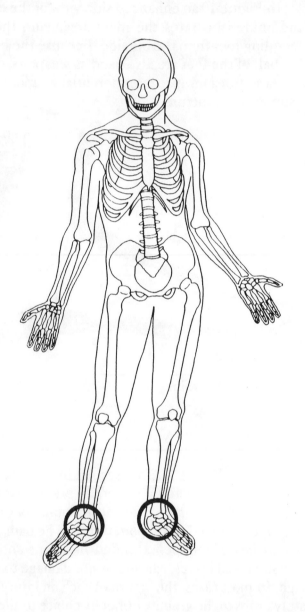

FIGURE 11   Target 2: Ankle

the injury by shutting down the muscles that flex to support the upright posture of the joint. In either case, the twisted ankle is not nearly as painful or debilitating as a thrust compression injury that would result from a forceful stomp or side kick.

In Figure 12, an enhanced illustration of the foot depicts the ankle abducted, or raised, as it would be if the calf (gastrocnemius) muscle were flexed. The tibia and fibula allow the ankle to glide beneath them so the foot can rise up onto its ball. This movement is required to push the body forward, backward, upward, or laterally.

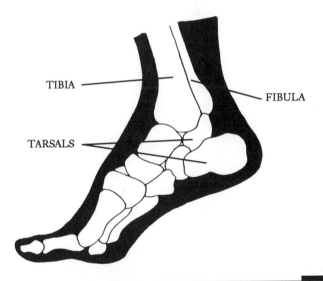

Bones around the Ankle   *FIGURE 12*

Specifically, your target is illustrated in Figure 13. The ankle is formed by the articulation of the tarsals, tibia, and fibula. This joint is required to support all or part of the body weight during the transition of weight while walking and running. When an ankle is effectively damaged, the leg is neutralized as a weight-bearing struc-

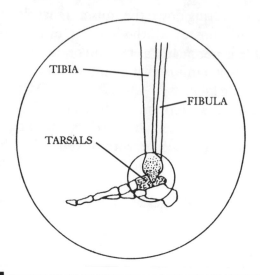

FIGURE 13

ture, thus rendering useless the corresponding lower quarter of the body.

Target Number 3: Knee

Observe Figure 14. Little emphasis needs to be placed on the importance of properly functioning knees. If you've ever seen a player get clipped on a football field, you can believe that he wasn't faking when he appeared to be totally consumed in agonizing pain from the injury.

Observe Figure 15. This is an enhanced front view of the formation of the knee. The femur descends from the hip, while the fibula and tibia ascend from the ankle to form this massive, free-moving joint. The kneecap (patella) rests at the tip of the femur. Figure 16 shows the back of the joint.

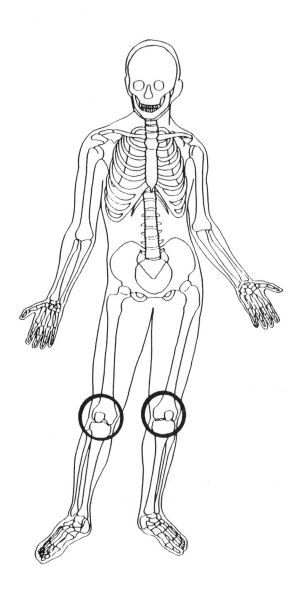

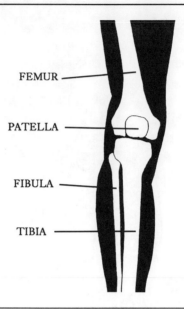

FEMUR

PATELLA

FIBULA

TIBIA

FIGURE 15 **Anterior View of Knee**

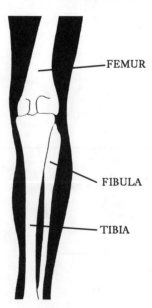

FEMUR

FIBULA

TIBIA

FIGURE 16 **Posterior View of Knee**

The ligamentation of the knee, as shown in Figure 17, is extensive and strong but equally vulnerable if your opponent is in the right position. The more freely a joint moves, the more intricate the ligamentation must be. The internal and external lateral ligaments are most readily damaged by impact forces. The anterior crucial ligament and transverse ligaments are generally damaged by a twisting movement.

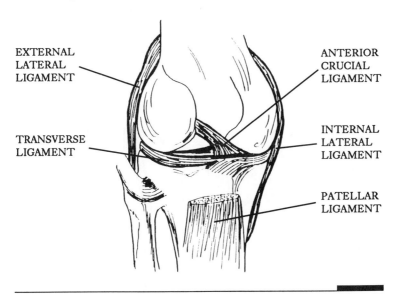

EXTERNAL LATERAL LIGAMENT

ANTERIOR CRUCIAL LIGAMENT

TRANSVERSE LIGAMENT

INTERNAL LATERAL LIGAMENT

PATELLAR LIGAMENT

Anterior View of External Knee Ligaments   *FIGURE 17*

Target Number 4: Fingers

Observe Figure 18. Like toes, fingers are relatively small bones, whose corresponding joints are free moving but weak. If you have ever bent a finger back too far, you know the immediate, debilitating pain that follows.

Figure 19, an enhanced illustration of the hand from a top view, depicts the many small bones of the wrist, hand,

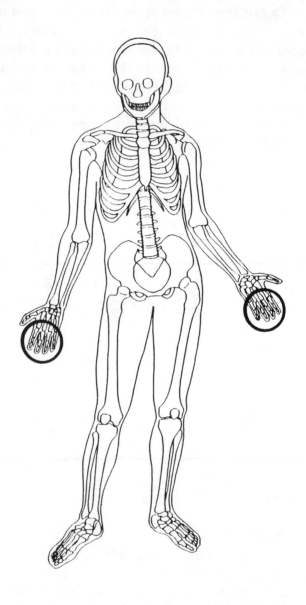

FIGURE 18   **Target 4: Fingers**

and fingers. Counting from the distal end (fingertips), the first three bones form the fingers (metacarpal phalanges); the thumb has only two bones. The metacarpals form the top of the hand.

Strategically, the hand and finger joints (indicated by an X) are best to target. The lengths of the fingers may be used as levers to put pressure on these particular joints, as opposed to other joints of the fingers that are more difficult to damage because of lack of leverage.

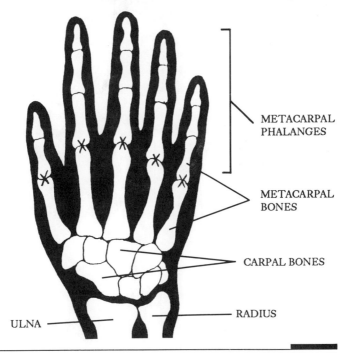

METACARPAL PHALANGES

METACARPAL BONES

CARPAL BONES

RADIUS

ULNA

Top View of Hand   *FIGURE 19*

Target Number 5: Wrist

Observe Figure 20. The similarities between the wrist (carpus) and ankle are evident from even a cursory

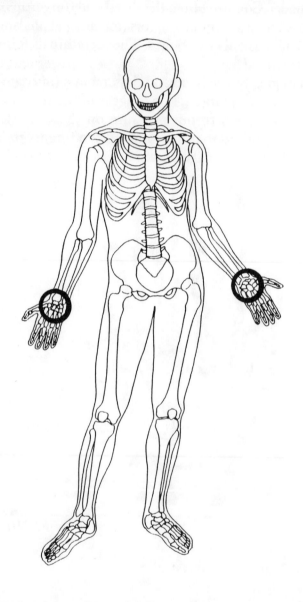

FIGURE 20 Target 5: Wrist

examination. Both are multifaceted with many small bones, both articulate with a pair of long bones, and both provide attachments for the corresponding bones that articulate the phalanges. Damaging the wrist would not complicate locomotion like damaging the ankle would, but it would put the corresponding arm out of action.

In Figure 21, the articulation of the wrists with the radius and ulna is highlighted by shading. As the ends of the fingers can be used as levers against their junction with the hands, the entire hand can be used as a lever against the wrist. The wrist may be damaged by hyperextending, hyperflexing, or hyper-rotating the joint in any direction.

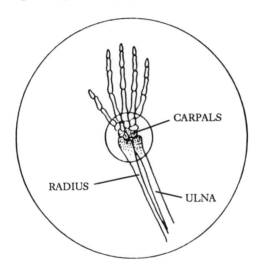

Articulation of Wrist   *FIGURE 21*

Target Number 6: Elbow

Observe Figure 22. Because the hands and arms are required to serve the body in countless ways, critical

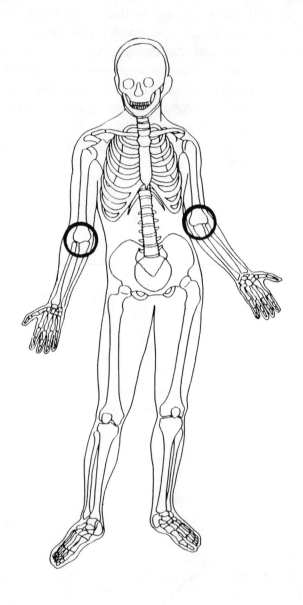

FIGURE 22   **Target 6: Elbow**

damage to the elbow will have serious, long-term effects. The immediate effect, similar to damaging a knee, is a quick end to a confrontation.

Three bones join at the elbow: the ulna, radius, and humerus. (Figure 23). The humerus, which occupies the upper portion of the arm, attaches to the scapula. The radius and the ulna join the humerus proximally and the carpus distally. (Re-examine Figures 3, 4, and 5.)

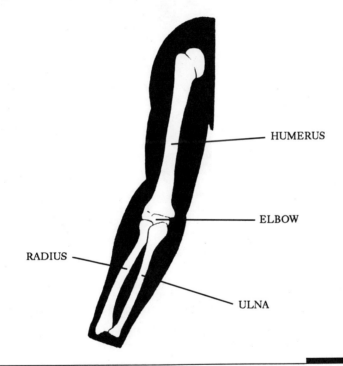

HUMERUS

ELBOW

RADIUS

ULNA

Elbow, Palm-up View   *FIGURE 23*

The elbow participates in the movement of the hand, which permits the palm to rotate upward or downward. In Figures 23 and 24, notice the difference in the position of the radius. In Figure 23, the radius is in the position corresponding with the palm-up position of the hand. In Figure 24, the radius crosses the ulna, corresponding with the palm-down position of the hand.

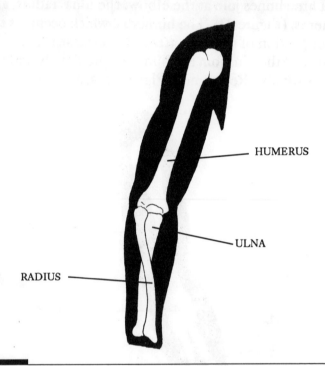

HUMERUS

ULNA

RADIUS

FIGURE 24   **Elbow, Palm-down View**

The elbow is most easily damaged by applying direct pressure to the dorsal, or back side, of the joint while trapping the hand or wrist. When the corresponding bones are extended beyond their range, the bone and cartilage are damaged as well as the ligament.

Target Number 7: Cervical Vertebrae

The seventh primary target is the cervical vertebrae, which are circled in Figure 25. This is the one target in

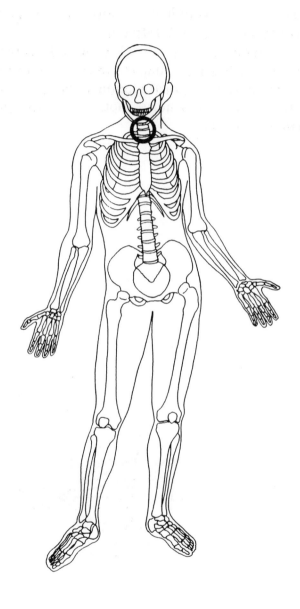

Target 7: Cervical Vertebrae *FIGURE 25*

this study that could be lethal. Therefore, we will spend a little more time analyzing its structure.

Observe Figure 26. This is a side view of the cervical vertebrae. As the illustration depicts, there are seven vertebrae composing the cervical section of the spinal column, with seven pairs of nerve roots exiting the cord through their foramina.

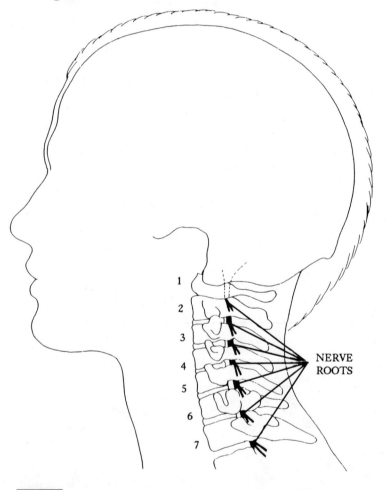

NERVE ROOTS

FIGURE 26   **Side View of Cervical Vertebrae**

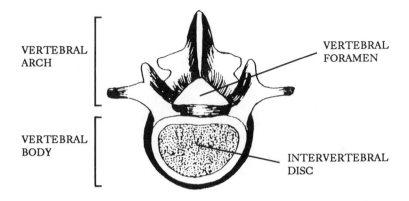

VERTEBRAL ARCH

VERTEBRAL FORAMEN

VERTEBRAL BODY

INTERVERTEBRAL DISC

FIGURE 27

Figure 27 illustrates the basic structure of a typical vertebra from a top-down view. The vertebral body is a curved, solid mass of bone, topped by an intervertebral disc that serves as a shock absorber for the vertebral body above it. At the rear of the body is the vertebral arch that forms a passage through which the spinal column descends to innervate the body. The rear angular view of the vertebra illustrated in Figure 28 provides a look at the

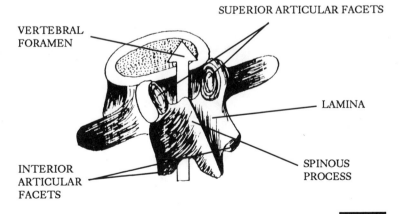

SUPERIOR ARTICULAR FACETS

VERTEBRAL FORAMEN

LAMINA

INTERIOR ARTICULAR FACETS

SPINOUS PROCESS

FIGURE 28

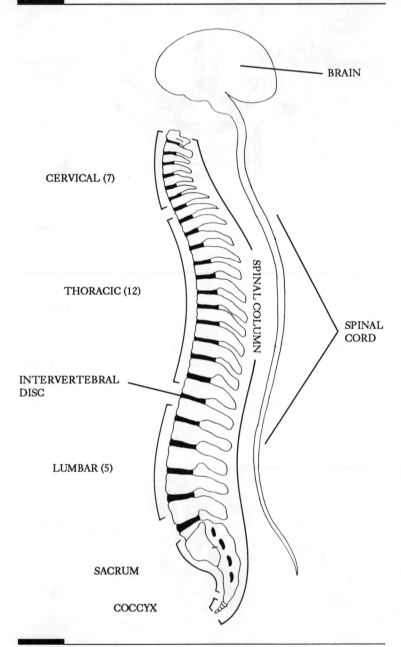

BRAIN

CERVICAL (7)

THORACIC (12)

SPINAL COLUMN

SPINAL CORD

INTERVERTEBRAL DISC

LUMBAR (5)

SACRUM

COCCYX

FIGURE 29

vertebral arch in greater detail. The superior articular facet provides a seat for the inferior articular facet of the vertebra above. When adjacent vertebrae align, the facets interlock. The lamina is the broad plate of bone on each side that fuses together to complete the arch. The pair of lamina, or laminae, encloses the spinal foramen, which protects the spinal cord. The spinous processes, one for each vertebra, descend from the junction of the laminae and direct the spinal cord down and to the rear. They also serve for muscle and ligamentation attachment.

Vertebrae serve many purposes for the body. Chief among them are the protection of the spinal cord and the distribution of the spinal nerves. In Figure 29, the spinal cord (nerve stem) and the spinal column (series of bones)

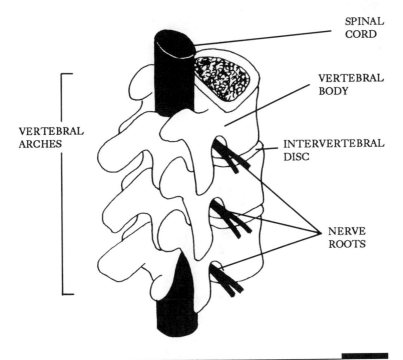

SPINAL CORD

VERTEBRAL BODY

VERTEBRAL ARCHES

INTERVERTEBRAL DISC

NERVE ROOTS

Cervical Nerve Distribution   *FIGURE 30*

are depicted adjacent to each other. The cord passes through the cervical, thoracic, lumbar, and sacral vertebrae, distributing a pair of nerves at the right and left through openings at each side of the vertebrae called intervertebral foramina. Figure 30 illustrates the nerve distribution process. It is these nerves that cause the cervical vertebrae to be such a lethal target.

Severely displaced or broken vertebrae can depress or sever the nerve roots passing through the intervertebral foramen. The nerves passing through the cervical section feed the heart and lungs. Simply put, damage to the cervical vertebrae could result in no innervation, no heartbeat, and no expansion or contraction of the lungs. Of course, death is not certain, but any attack here could easily result in quadriplegia.

Finally, as depicted in Figure 31, the cervical vertebrae support the weight of the head, a function which also makes them a highly lethal target.

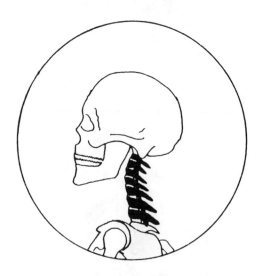

FIGURE 31   Side View of Cervical Vertebrae

• • • • •

These are your seven primary targets for guge gongji. In the chapters covering practical application, we will learn how to attack other anatomical targets and how to use prestrike blocks as lead-ins or set-up maneuvers to get to these secondary targets. However, the focus of your concentration should be on the methods and angles for striking these seven primary targets. Guge gongji teaches you how to control the biomechanical functions of an opponent's body by interrupting its locomotion and thus neutralizing it as a threat. Keep the purpose of the study in mind.

CHAPTER THREE

Recognizing Joint Posture Vulnerability

In this chapter, we're going to look at our seven primary targets from an external perspective to study their most vulnerable postures. As a rule, joints are most readily damaged when their abductors are fully flexed and, in the case of the central joints of the limbs, when they are being held at their furthest point from the midline of the body. Learning to recognize these vulnerable postures may someday prove invaluable.

Bridge of the Foot and Toes

In Figure 32, the shaded circle represents the target area. The arrow depicts the line of drive to apply in attacking the target. In this illustration, the opponent's left foot would be closest to you if you were facing him and would, therefore, be more vulnerable.

The bridge of the foot (metatarsals) and the toes (metatarsal phalanges) are most useful as targets in

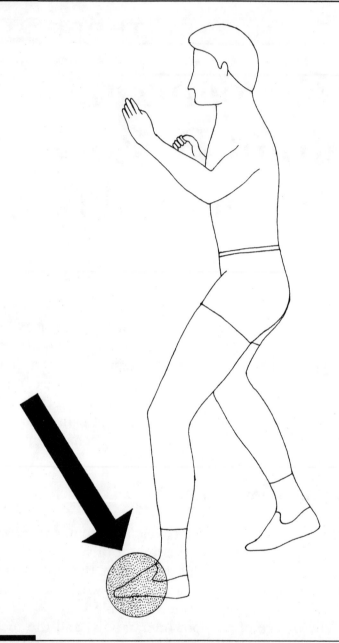

FIGURE 32 **Attacking the Bridge of the Foot**

clinches or other close-contact situations, especially when an opponent has approached and grappled you from behind. Rear bear hugs over or under the arms, a full nelson, and one-arm chokeholds are typical rear-hold attacks. Except in rare instances, an opponent's feet will be in the immediate proximity of your own when he has put an offensive hold on you. A firm stomp on one or both feet will at least buy you a few moments to initiate another defensive action while the opponent is occupied with the pain you have caused him. If, during the course of a confrontation, one of your opponent's feet gets close enough to yours and you can safely get to the target without exposing yourself to an incoming blow, you should take advantage of the opportunity. An opponent's balance and mobility will be substantially diminished when he is standing on a broken foot, making him easier to defeat. By damaging a foot, you are taking out an anatomical weapon and reducing your opponent's arsenal.

The Ankle

The ankle (tarsus) is a multifaceted joint that, unlike the foot and fingers, is relied upon by the appendicular skeleton to support 50 percent of the weight of the entire torso. An opponent with broken toes or a broken bridge can still support his weight by shifting it onto the heel; one with a severely damaged ankle cannot. When you have broken an opponent's ankle, you have immobilized him.

Observe Figure 33. This opponent's ankle is considerably forward of his midline and is his closest anatomical target to you. A down-thrusting side kick in the direction

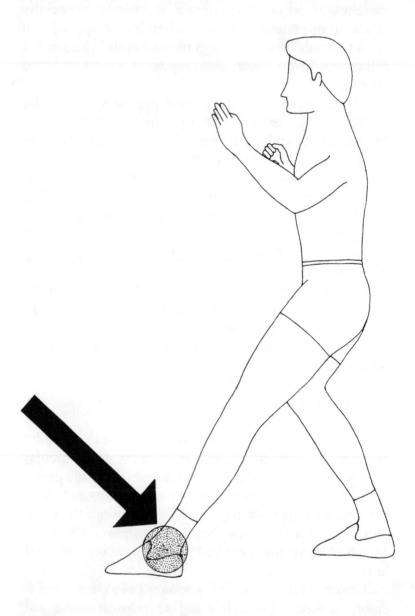

FIGURE 33

Targeting the Ankle

indicated by the arrow could stop the confrontation without further exchange.

Some martial arts teach this stance or a variation of it as a bait-in. It is also a strategic position that is sometimes used in conjunction with a low hand profile, appearing to leave the face unprotected. When an opponent perceives that the upper-torso targets are open to attack and makes a forward lunge to strike them, you can counterstrike with the lead foot. Because the foot is being held low and close to the opponent's body, a strike initiated from it has an increased chance of landing effectively without interference.

In Figure 34, the opponent is depicted out of position; you are behind him. When the ankle is fully adducted (or brought forward) as shown here, the ligaments are already stretched to their full capacity. The facets of the tarsal bones are also at their extreme range. A down-thrusting side kick applied in the direction and approximate area indicated by the arrow will force the joint beyond its capacity and damage its facets and ligamentation.

The ankle may also be attacked with the line of thrust indicated in Figure 33, but force should be applied from either the inside or outside of the joint.

Note that the attack in Figure 33 is mechanically different than the attack in Figure 34. The method used in Figure 33 is to apply striking force directly to the target area, causing the damage by impact force. The method used in Figure 34 is a leveraged application of force. The blow is not being directed to the target itself but rather to an adjoining bone, using it as a lever to take the joint beyond its normal capacity. You will encounter these differences throughout the remainder of this chapter and in the chapters on technical application.

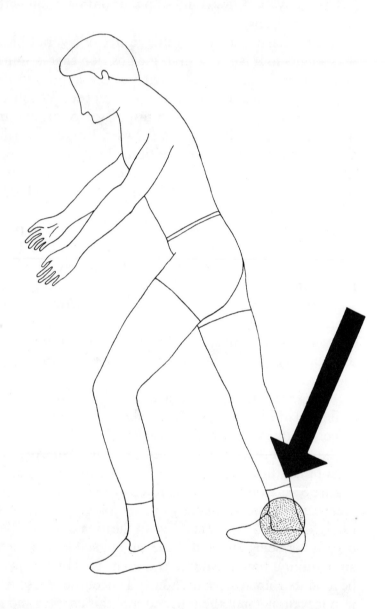

FIGURE 34   Targeting the Ankle from the Rear

The Knee

If you have ever had the misfortune of injuring your knee or just smacking your kneecap on the corner of a coffee table, causing temporary pain, you can appreciate the effects of a strike to the knee. When dealing with the knee as a target, you are going far beyond the structural implications and the relative dependency upon the joint for appendicular support. The intensity of pain associated with traumatic injury to the knee is completely, unconditionally, and instantaneously debilitating. It is also the most overlooked target on the human torso.

Inexperienced fighters tend to be "headhunters," discounting most mid- and lower-body targets. But even body punchers will generally pass up prime shots to the knee. The shame of it is that the knees, while being critical targets, are extremely difficult to defend. If you learn nothing else from this study, remember that the knees are primary targets in personal combat— keep *yours* protected.

Observe Figure 35. This opponent's right side is toward you, exposing the outside of the knee. A low, thrusting side kick that follows the line of force indicated by the arrow will cause crucial damage to the ligaments maintaining the bones that form the knee joint.

In Figure 36, the opponent is standing in an upright position facing you head-on. A straight kick (indicated by the dotted arrow) or a down-thrusting kick (following the black arrow) will critically damage the knee.

Observe Figure 37. For the experienced fighter, the position of the opponent's lead leg is a victory on a silver platter. A firm side kick that follows the line of force indicated by the arrow will literally destroy this opponent's left knee. You couldn't find an opponent's knee more per-

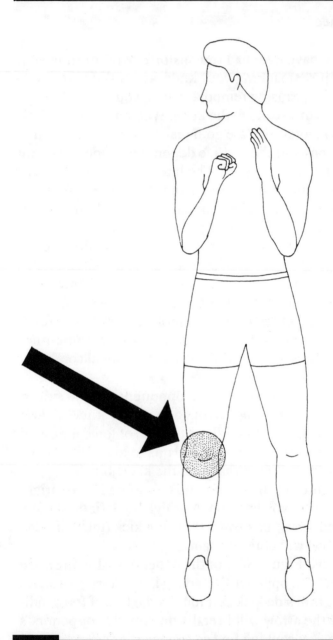

FIGURE 35   Knee as an Outside Target

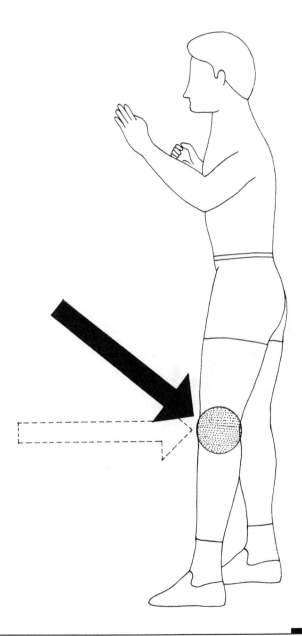

Knee as a Frontal Target   *FIGURE 36*

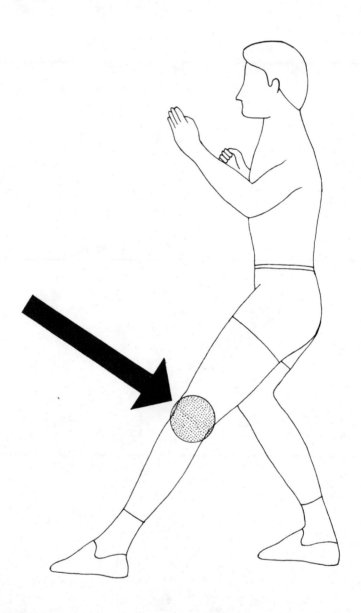

FIGURE 37   **Perfect Position for Knee Attack**

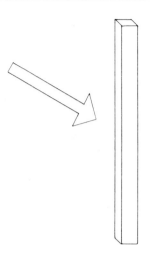

Absorption of Force *FIGURE 38*

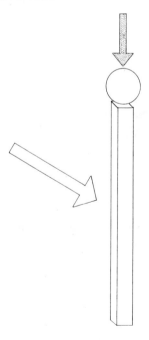

With Weight Added *FIGURE 39*

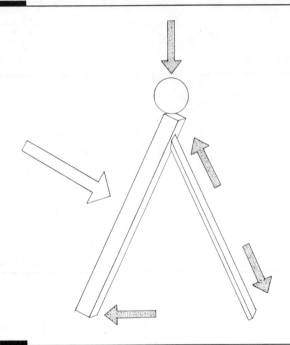

FIGURE 40   **With Weight and Resistance Added**

fectly positioned for an attack while he is standing unless he were in this same position with his back against a wall.

Observe Figure 38. Picture this piece of wood as a target, standing on its edge as depicted. Absorption of impact force (for more information, see *Iron Hand of the Dragon's Touch*, available from Paladin Press) is an important factor in determining how much damage will result from a thrust effort. A 500-pound thrust against the board may do little more than send the board flying across a room. Now look at Figure 39. The weight on top of the board provides resistance to the incoming effort, causing the board to absorb more of the total impact force applied. Now look at Figure 40, an inanimate representation of the opponent's posture illustrated in Figure 37.

Here you have resistance pushing downward (opponent's body weight), resistance at the base of the board because of its angle and the angle of the incoming thrust (opponent's posture relative to the thrusting effort), and additional resistance from the thinner board at the rear of the target (opponent's rear leg). Which of these three figures—38, 39, or 40—will absorb more of the incoming force from the thrust? Figure 40 has the most support (resistance) and will therefore absorb more of the incoming thrust and sustain the greatest amount of damage.

Figure 41 represents an opponent with his back against a wall; this position allows no give at either end of the board, thereby forcing him to absorb 100 percent of the incoming impact force.

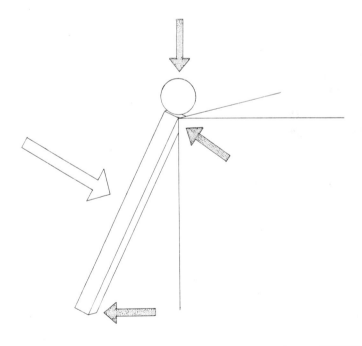

Maximum Force Absorption   *FIGURE 41*

The position depicted in Figure 37 is about as ideal as you could expect in a moving confrontation, and the knee should be considered a priority target. At this angle, extensive, debilitating damage would occur from a properly delivered thrust.

The Fingers

The fingers (metacarpal phalanges) are considerably more accessible as targets than the toes; fingers have too many vulnerable positions to show. Anytime an opponent's hands are in a grappling position on your neck, shoulders, arms, wrists, or other part of your body, they are vulnerable. When an opponent's fingers are abducted from the palm in an open position, they can easily be bent backward toward the top of the hand, snapping one or more of the joints binding the bones together. The fifth metacarpal phalanx (pinky finger) is the most easily broken of the fingers because of its small bones.

Observe Figure 42. During an intense physical confrontation, combatants often fall to the ground in a variety of positions.

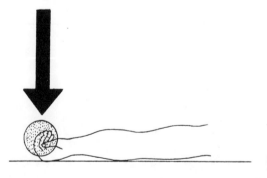

FIGURE 42   **The Fingers as Targets**

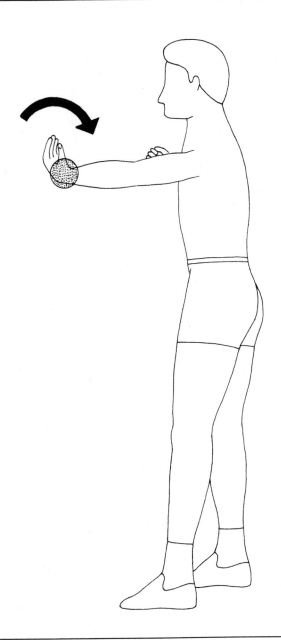

The Wrist as Target *FIGURE 43*

If you should find your opponent's hand in this position, stomp on top of the fingers to neutralize that hand
as a weapon or grappling tool. An equally vulnerable target is a hand held palm-down with the fingers folded
beneath it.

The Wrist

The wrist is one of the most fluid joints of the body
and is vulnerable in a variety of positions. The position
depicted in Figure 43 shows the hand fully adducted, or
bent *toward* the inside of the forearm. Forcing the hand
in the direction shown by the arrow hyperflexes the
carpal bones beyond their capacity, causing damage to
the ligaments as well as to the bones themselves.

Applying direct pressure to the carpal bones, such as
in a strike, is ineffective because it is difficult to brace the
hand against the absorption of impact force. The best
way to attack the wrist is to use the hand as a lever to
force the wrist to hyperflex, hyperextend, or rotate
beyond its design.

From the position depicted in Figure 43, you can
rotate the hand clockwise or counterclockwise, putting
pressure on the wrist at the junction of the carpal bones
and the ulnar/radial joint. Applying pressure at medium
speed stretches the joint, yielding only minor, temporary
incapacitation. Applying full-force pressure at high speed
causes major damage, and some of that damage probably
will be permanent.

The Elbow

The elbow is a major weapon in the art of personal
combat that, when properly applied, has devastating

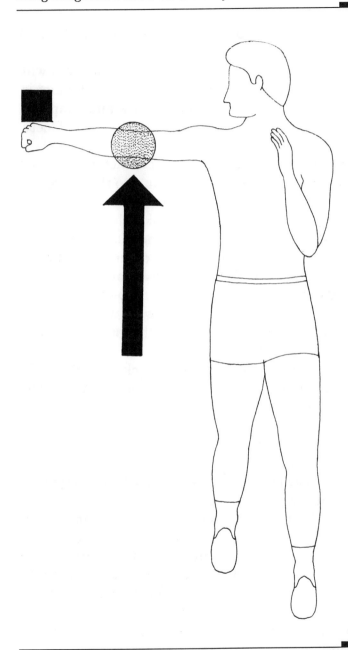

Attacking an Extended Elbow *FIGURE 44*

impact force. It is also a strong joint, unless the arm is extended.

Figure 44 depicts the vulnerable position you will encounter most frequently for the elbow. The arm is extended from throwing a punch. Block-and-wrap and arm-trapping techniques use the elbow as a point of focus for their debilitating maneuvers.

Look at the arrow in Figure 44. It depicts your line of drive for attacking the elbow. Notice also that there is a block illustrated over the top of the hand. A drive could be applied without securing the end of the arm, but the effort would yield only a fraction of the results that would be achieved by blocking the hand or wrist during the drive. You may also apply a line of drive downward on the end of the arm while applying rising pressure to the elbow. The downward drive at the wrist would serve as an enhanced block while increasing the total force of the movement.

Whenever you find the elbow locked in the fully abducted position, it is vulnerable to an assortment of attacks that will be discussed in later chapters.

Cervical Vertebrae

The cervical vertebrae, as we learned in Chapter 2, are the one target in this study that, properly attacked, could yield fatal consequences. Even seemingly less severe attacks can cause paralysis in varying degrees.

Generally, striking the vertebrae, such as with a shuto or a hook kick, will do minimal damage unless the attacker applies deep penetration at high speed. The most damaging attacks to this area are those that use the cranium and maxilla as levers to force the vertebrae beyond their capacity to flex or rotate.

Backward Cervical Thrust   *FIGURE 45*

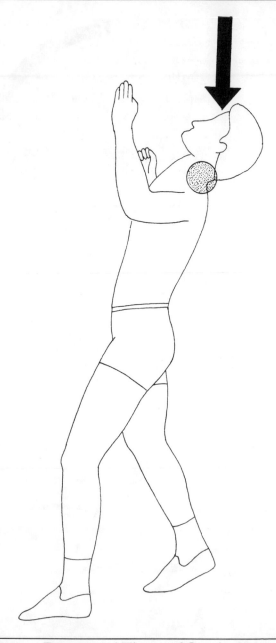

FIGURE 46   Downward Thrust of Cervical Vertebrae

The most vulnerable cervical posture you will likely encounter in moving combat is the hyperextended posture illustrated in Figures 45 and 46. In Figure 45, the head and neck are rolled backward, extending the cervical vertebrae to their fullest rear capacity. By applying a push-drive force in the direction of the arrow, the articulating facets of the third through sixth vertebrae either slip from their positions or snap completely. A deep drive yields the latter result.

In Figure 46, the head and neck are in the same position, but the arrow indicating the line of drive is quite different. With the head in this position, a line of drive following the black arrow breaks the articulating facets of the atlas (first cervical vertebra attached to the base of the cranium) and the axis (second cervical vertebra adjoining the atlas). The probability of surviving such a stroke is about nil, and anyone who did survive would be a quadriplegic. This strike should be used only to save another life—including your own—since it is fatal the majority of the time.

When the head is held upright and rotated fully to the right or left, the chin-lever rotation technique, which we will discuss in later chapters, has the same effect on the cervical vertebrae as the strike illustrated in Figure 45 if applied at a controlled depth (up to four inches). If the chin travels beyond four inches during the attack, nerve root damage or separation occurs—with fatal consequences.

CHAPTER FOUR

Targets below the Waist

The inferior transverse plane is the lower half of the body. The surgical application would include the hands because they hang below the waist, but the wrists and fingers will be discussed in the next chapter. Here, we will study single-stroke attacks to the toes, bridges of the feet, ankles, and knees.

You must pay as much attention to the starting positions for each of these techniques as you do to the attacks. This will help you to recognize vulnerable postures during movement and allow you to maneuver from your opponent's attacks more efficiently.

In every illustration where either combatant is depicted in an advanced position, a shadow figure depicting the previous position has been added to help you visualize the movement more clearly. Keep the lessons learned in the previous chapters in mind as you progress through these techniques.

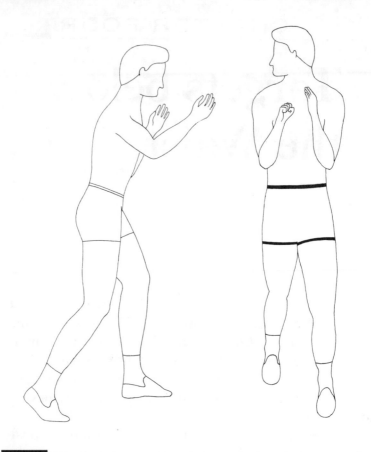

FIGURE 47

Feet and Toes

Figures 47 through 49

Figure 47. For the remainder of this text, you will be depicted wearing the trunks with the dark trim. In this illustration, your opponent is approaching from your right side and reaching for the upper quarter of your body with his right hand.

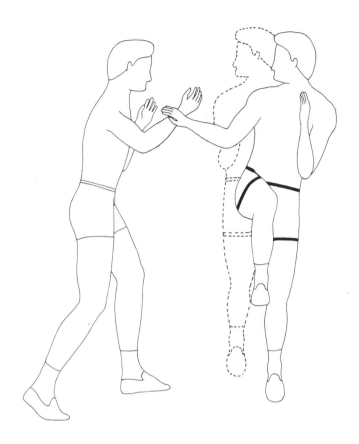

FIGURE 48

Figure 48. In a simultaneous motion, shift your body weight onto your left leg and chamber your right foot for a low side kick. As you shift into this position, use a sweeping shuto block to stop the advance of your opponent's hand.

Figure 49. Again in simultaneous motion, bring your body weight toward your opponent and stomp your right foot down on the bridge of his right foot. As you execute

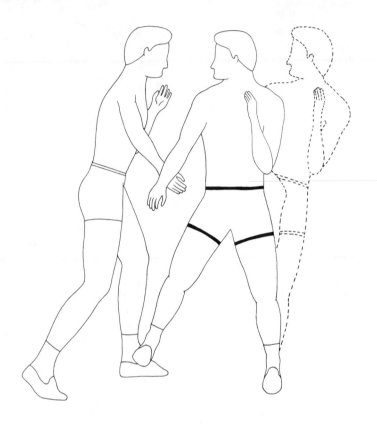

FIGURE 49

the counterstrike, slip the palm of your blocking hand onto the top of your opponent's offending wrist and push it forcefully downward. Be sure your hand remains to the *outside* of his as shown. If your arm positions get reversed, your opponent could strike your face more easily.

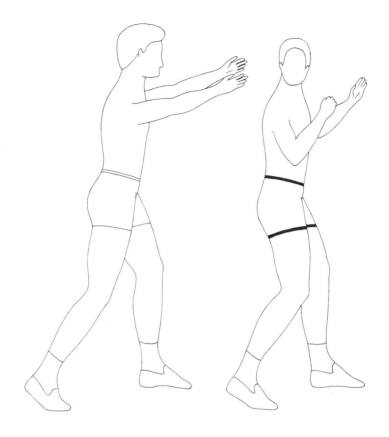

FIGURE 50

Figures 50 through 52

Figure 50. Here your opponent is approaching from your rear and reaching with both hands for your head.

Figure 51. Shift your body weight onto your left leg and chamber your right foot for a low rear kick. You will note that by shifting onto your left foot and tilting the upper body slightly forward, you move your opponent's intended target out of his reach.

FIGURE 51

Figure 52. Drive your body weight in your opponent's direction with your left leg and stomp down on the toes or bridge of his foot with your right foot.

(See also *Danger Zones: Defending Yourself against Surprise Attack*, available from Paladin Press, for alternative rear defenses.)

FIGURE 52

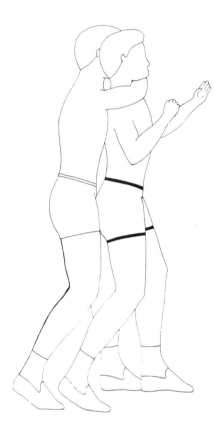

FIGURE 53

Figures 53 through 56

Figure 53. In this illustration, your opponent has gotten behind you and grabbed you with a one-armed choke. While an opponent is holding you around the neck from the rear, you are in considerable danger. You must respond to grappling attacks quickly and, preferably, reflexively. (In an earlier Paladin book, *Master's Guide to Basic Self-Defense*, I discussed instinct and reflex training in detail.)

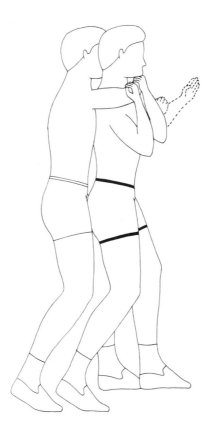

FIGURE 54

Figure 54. The first movement of this sequence may not always be necessary. Some rear chokeholds do not actually constrict the airway. If the grip around your neck is not preventing normal breathing, you may eliminate this move without consequence. However, if the opponent's arm is limiting your ability to breathe, reach up with both hands as indicated and jerk down forcefully to move his arm so you can breathe.

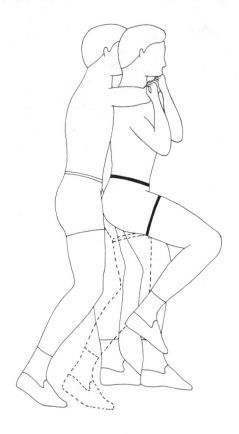

FIGURE 55

Figure 55. Still holding onto his arm, draw your right foot up to the position shown.

Figure 56. Stomp down forcefully on your opponent's toes or the bridge of his right foot. Make sure this is a maximum power effort; you may not get a second chance to execute it. Any number of follow-up techniques, which I have outlined in previous books, may be used after this blow.

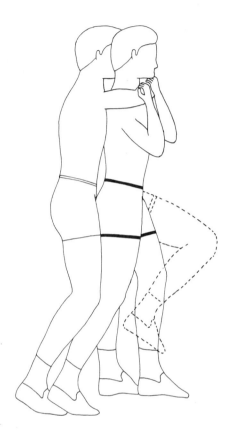

FIGURE 56

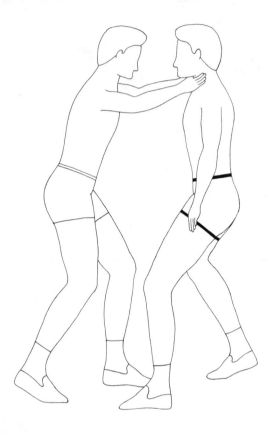

FIGURE 57

Figures 57 through 60

Figure 57. The front two-handed choke is a common street attack. It always entails impairment of breathing.

Figure 58. The movements in the next three steps of this technique must be performed quickly. Reach up with both hands, tightly grappling your opponent's wrists.

Figure 59. As you clamp onto your opponent's wrists,

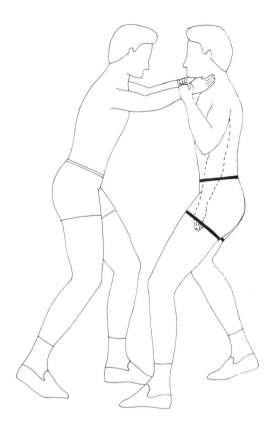

FIGURE 58

raise your right leg to the position shown, *outside* of his left leg.

Figure 60. With your toes pointing out to your right, stomp your right heel down forcefully onto the bridge of your opponent's left foot. Keep in mind that all attacks to the bridge of the foot also may be directed at the toes.

FIGURE 59

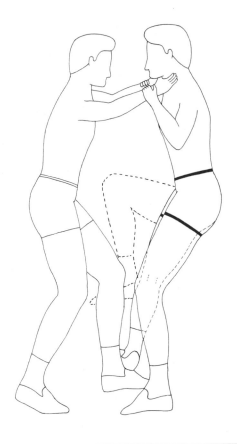

FIGURE 60

FIGURE 61

The Ankle

Figures 61 through 64
Figure 61. You are squared off with your opponent in a face-to-face position.

Figure 62. In this first frame, your opponent has leaned forward, extending a long, right-hand punch. With your right hand, you have made a left-to-right circu-

FIGURE 62

lar sweep, redirecting the incoming punch to the outside of your body.

Figure 63. Push your opponent's offending hand down and with a slight hop align your left heel with your opponent's left foot, while drawing up your right leg to a low chamber position.

Figure 64. Using your body weight to assist the thrust, stomp down on the front side of your opponent's

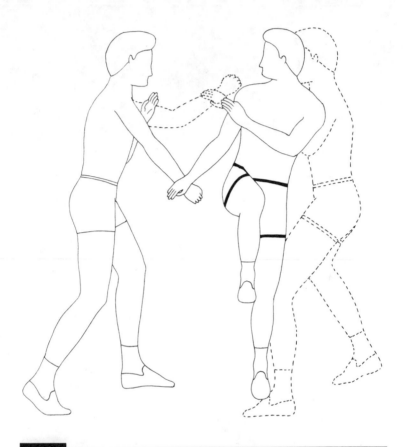

FIGURE 63

ankle. Note the position of your left leg. Bending this leg
as you thrust your kick will add power to the stroke.

FIGURE 64

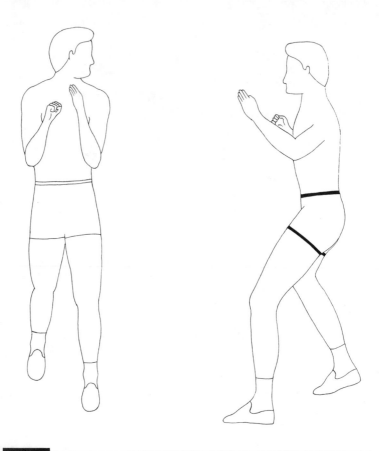

FIGURE 65

Figures 65 through 67

Figure 65. In this sequence you will be starting on your opponent's left side.

Figure 66. Again, you have advanced toward your opponent simply by shifting your body weight onto and rotating your left foot. The right leg is drawn up to the chamber position for a low side kick.

Figure 67. This time you strike the ankle from the

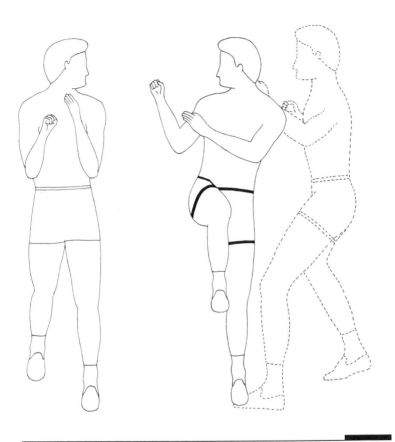

FIGURE 66

outside. The thrust and technique are the same as the previous sequence.

FIGURE 67

FIGURE 68

Figures 68 through 71

Figure 68. Again, you begin with your opponent at your north gate (front, facing).

Figure 69. Your opponent leads with a leaning right-hand punch directed toward your face. You redirect the blow with a left-to-right circular shuto block.

Figure 70. Instead of forcing the opponent's hand downward as in previous techniques, clamp his right

FIGURE 69

wrist tightly with your blocking hand and shift your
weight onto your left leg, chambering your right foot for a
low side kick.

Figure 71. Note the slight shift of your left foot. You
are striking the inside of your opponent's ankle, requir-
ing a slight rotation of the standing heel as shown. As you
deliver the kick, push the opponent's trapped arm down

FIGURE 70

and across his body, neutralizing any chance of his using either hand to strike you.

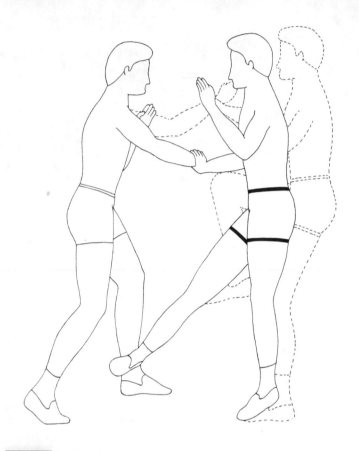

FIGURE 71

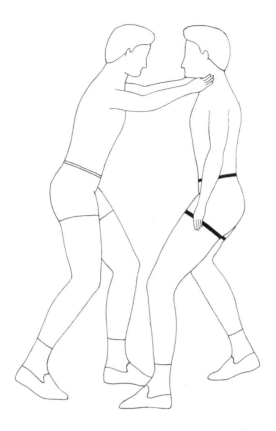

FIGURE 72

Figures 72 through 75

Figure 72. Here your opponent has grabbed you with a two-handed front choke.

Figure 73. Again, your first move is to get a firm grip on both of your opponent's wrists.

Figure 74. Note the slight counterclockwise step with the left foot. This is to facilitate the final stroke. The right foot has been chambered for a low side kick.

FIGURE 73

Figure 75. Extend a hard-driven side kick to the inside of your opponent's left ankle.

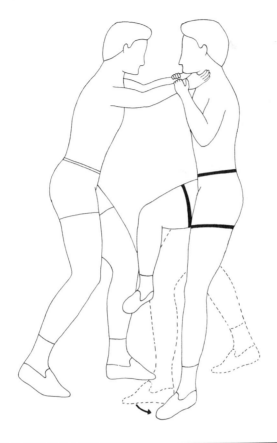

FIGURE 74

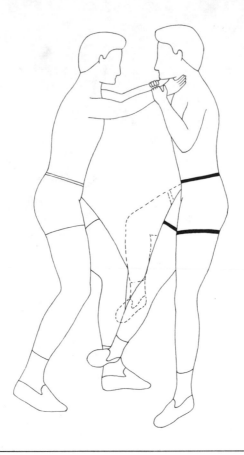

FIGURE 75

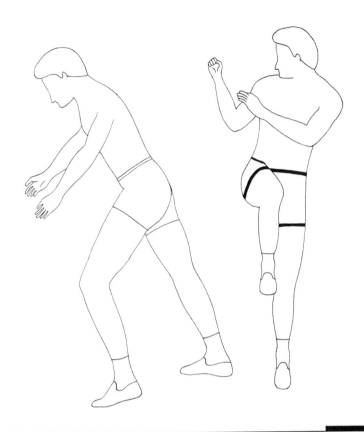

FIGURE 76

Figures 76 through 79

These low side kick applications to the ankle illustrate attacks corresponding with the vulnerable positions discussed in Chapter 3.

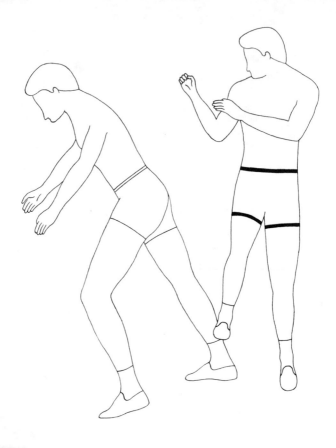

FIGURE 77

FIGURE 78

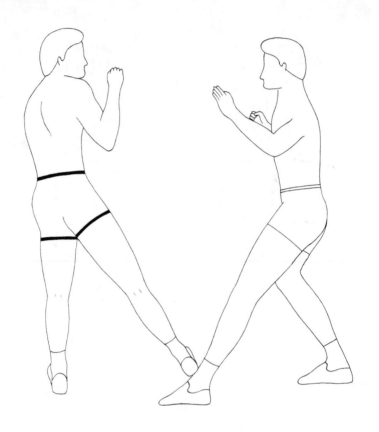

FIGURE 79

FIGURE 80

The Knee

Figures 80 through 82

Figure 80. Starting in a front-facing position, you will initiate the first move.

Figure 81. Without stepping, bring your weight forward onto your left foot, rotate counterclockwise, and chamber your right leg for a low side kick.

FIGURE 81

Figure 82. Putting your body weight into the thrust, snap your side kick into your opponent's left knee.

FIGURE 82

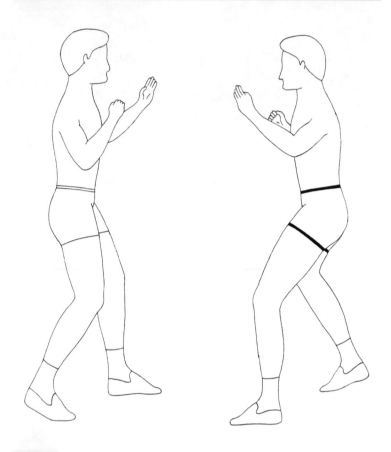

FIGURE 83

Figures 83 through 86

Figure 83. Beginning again from a facing position, this technique requires a skill level at which you are able to move quickly and accurately.

Figure 84. Your opponent has brought his weight forward onto his left foot to close the gap between you.

Figure 85. Take a short, quick step forward and to the outside of the span of your opponent's right stance. As

FIGURE 84

you make this step, simultaneously palm block the incoming right punch while chambering your right leg.

Figure 86. With a slight rotation of the left foot, extend your side kick into the inside of your opponent's right knee.

FIGURE 85

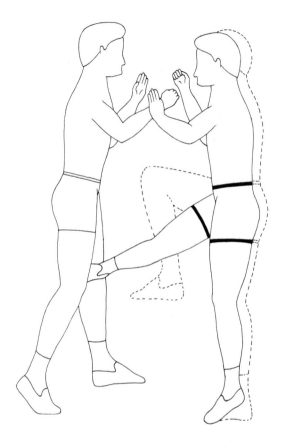

FIGURE 86

FIGURE 87

Figures 87 through 89

Figure 87. Begin from a face-to-face, in-stance position with your opponent.

Figure 88. Your opponent has begun a right-hand lead punch to your upper quarter, tilting his stance forward to close the gap. You have shuffled your left foot counterclockwise, shifting your weight onto that foot while chambering your right foot for a low side kick. Because

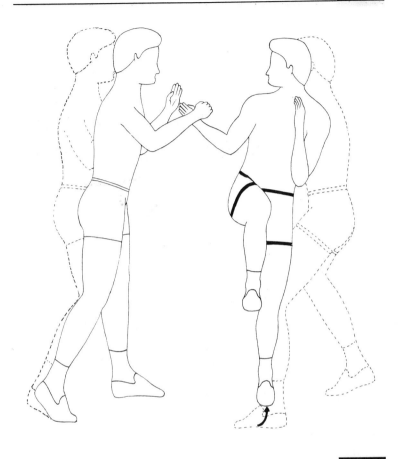

FIGURE 88

you are moving to the inside of the incoming punch, you use an inside palm block to control the stroke.

Figure 89. Extend your right side kick into the front of your opponent's left knee.

FIGURE 89

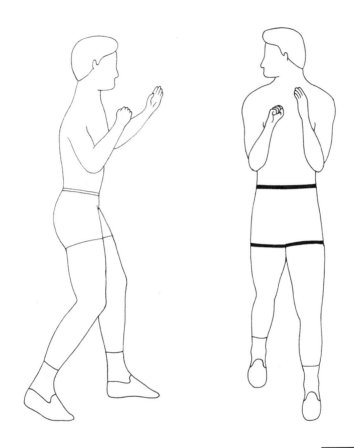

FIGURE 90

Figures 90 through 93

Figure 90. In this final sequence, your opponent is positioned in a fighting stance at your east gate.

Figure 91. Here your opponent has again leaned forward and reached out with a right-hand punch directed at your upper quarter.

Figure 92. Shifting your weight onto your left leg, draw your right leg to the chamber position and open

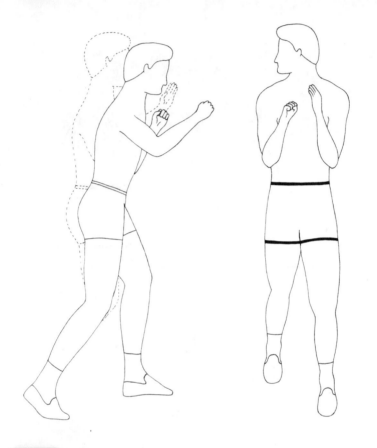

FIGURE 91

your right hand to trap the fist of your opponent's incoming arm.

Figure 93. Cupping your opponent's fist, extend a driving side kick into the front of his knee.

FIGURE 92

FIGURE 93

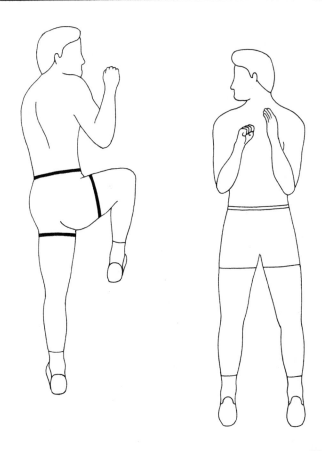

FIGURE 94

Figures 94 through 99
These illustrations depict the low side kick applied to the vulnerable positions for the knee discussed in Chapter 3.

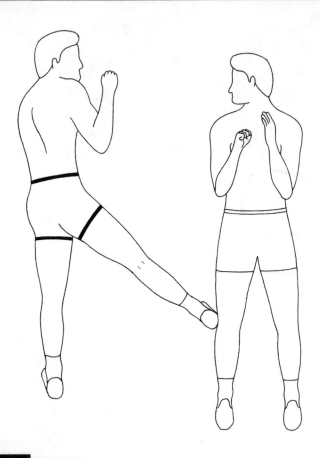

FIGURE 95

FIGURE 96

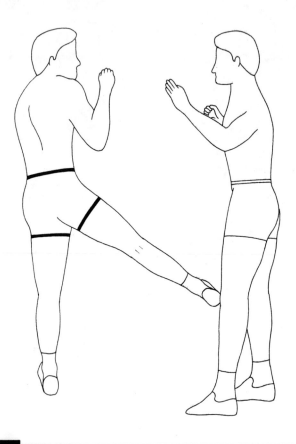

FIGURE 97

FIGURE 98

FIGURE 99

CHAPTER FIVE

Targets above the Waist

I n this chapter, we will study upper-torso (upper transverse plane) targets—specifically, the fingers, wrists, and elbows. The cervical vertebrae will be treated separately. The majority of your counterstrikes will be executed with upper-body weapons, as opposed to the counterstrikes in Chapter 4.

There are no rules dictating that upper-body targets should be attacked with upper-body weapons and lower-body targets attacked with lower-body weapons. Of course, speed is a factor. The shorter the distance between a weapon and its target, the less the time it will take to make contact.

Deception also can be a factor in the selection of targets. For example, a hand strike to the knee would be as unexpected as a hook kick to the temple. Although distances affect delivery time, these types of techniques are not impractical under the appropriate circumstances. However, we will concentrate primarily on efficiency, so most of your counterattacks will correspond with target/weapon regions.

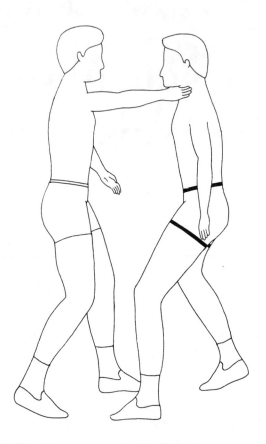

FIGURE 100

The Fingers

Figures 100 through 102

Figure 100. In this illustration, your opponent has taken a grip on your neck, choking you with his right hand.

Figure 101. Reach up with your left hand, force your first two fingers (index and middle) under your opponent's pinky finger, and hold the finger tightly.

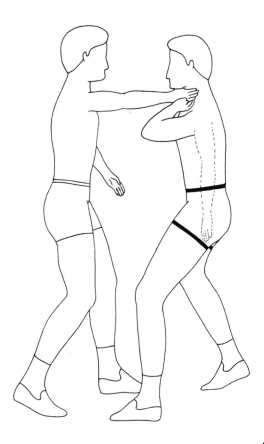

FIGURE 101

Figure 102. With a quick snapping motion, bend the finger out and down, pulling your opponent's hand off your neck. The snap, if properly executed, will break your opponent's pinky knuckle.

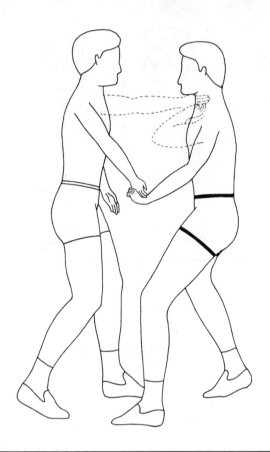

FIGURE 102

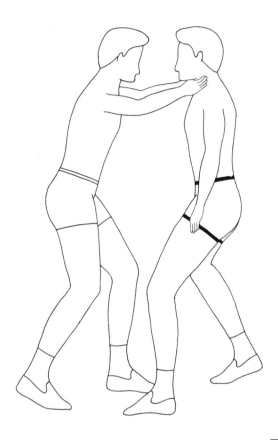

FIGURE 103

Figures 103 through 105

Figure 103. Your starting position is a two-handed front choke attack.

Figure 104. Using the same method of grappling the pinky finger, pry your first and second fingers under the pinky fingers of both your opponent's hands. Get a tight grip.

Figure 105. Simultaneously snap both pinky fingers

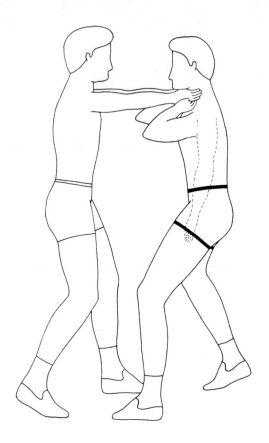

FIGURE 104

back toward your opponent's body. Again, proper execution of the snap will break the knuckle joints of each finger.

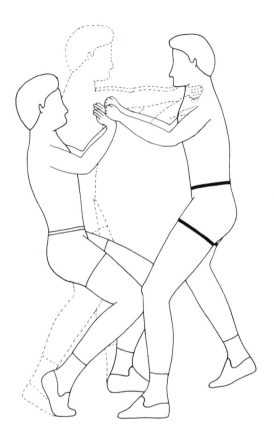

FIGURE 105

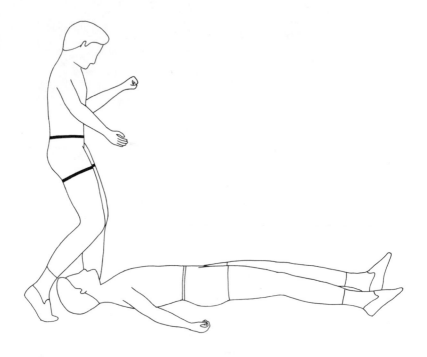

FIGURE 106

Figures 106 through 108

Figure 106. As a finishing target, the fingers provide a bad memory for an opponent you have encountered. Here your adversary is down from a previously executed technique.

Figure 107. Raise your right foot as depicted.

Figure 108. Using the strength of your leg and body weight, stomp down on the partially bent fingers of your

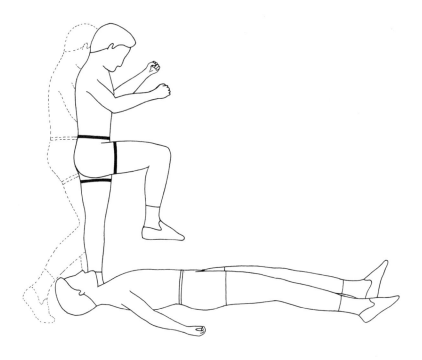

FIGURE 107

opponent. If the hand is faced palm-down, the effects of the stomp are the same: numerous breaks in the joints and/or bones of the fingers and hand.

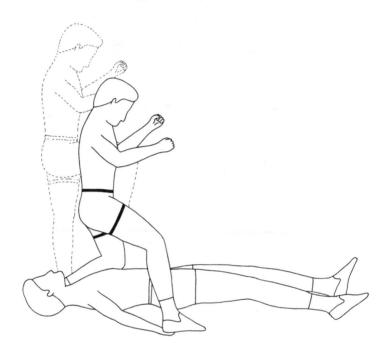

FIGURE 108

The Wrist

The wrist is most useful as a target during grappling attacks and, as you will see, can be used as a takedown or throwing lever.

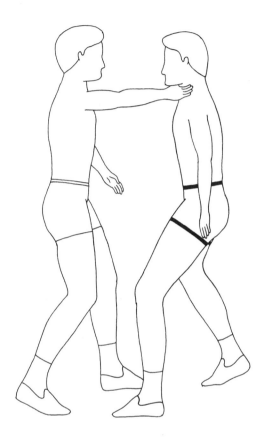

FIGURE 109

Figures 109 through 113

Figure 109. You are again beginning from a one-hand choke attack.

Figures 110 and 111. Reach across your face and over the top of your opponent's arm with your right hand and force your fingers under his hand, achieving the grip depicted in Figure 111.

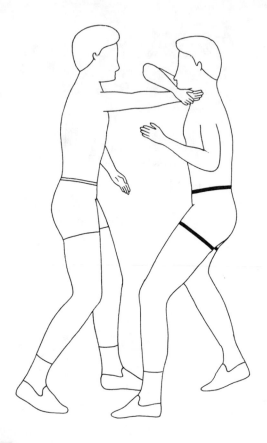

FIGURE 110

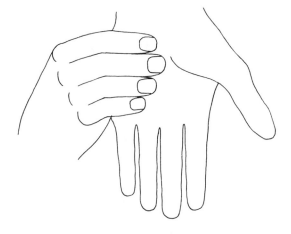

FIGURE 111

FIGURE 112

Figures 112 and 113. Peel your opponent's hand off your neck by rotating his hand clockwise and bringing it to the center of your chest. His elbow will rotate upward, putting pressure on the wrist. Immediately take a second grip on his hand with your left hand (Figure 113). Bend his wrist toward his hand. Your thumbs should cross on the back of his hand. Again, each of these movements is executed with a snapping motion.

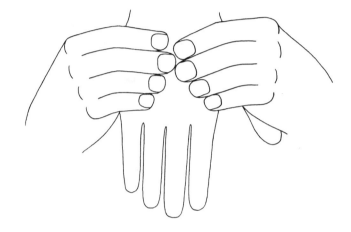

FIGURE 113

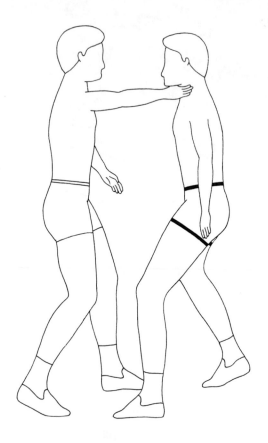

FIGURE 114

Figures 114 through 118

Figures 114 and 115. We will work from the same attack and use the same basic defensive maneuver, but we are going to change the direction of the lever.

Figures 116 and 117. The opponent's hand is again rotated clockwise and given reinforcement with the left hand.

Figure 118. Now go back to Figure 112. In that illus-

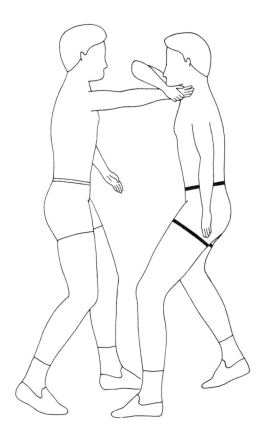

FIGURE 115

tration, the aggressor's upper body remained upright. In Figure 118, he tilts forward. Notice the arrows depicting the line of drive. By changing the direction in which the pressure is applied, you change the opponent's reaction to the effort. Carefully study the reactions depicted in the following illustrations.

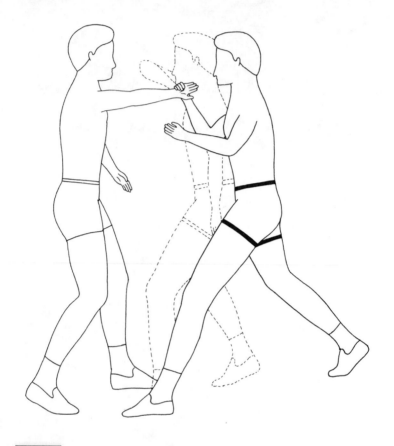

FIGURE 116

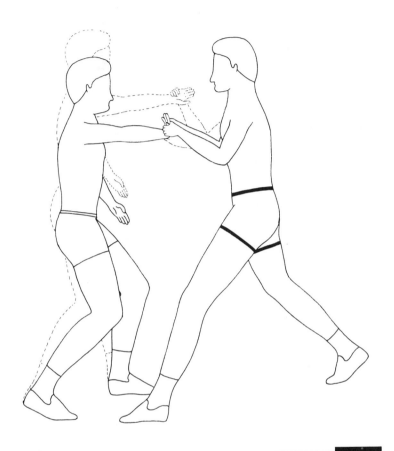

FIGURE 117

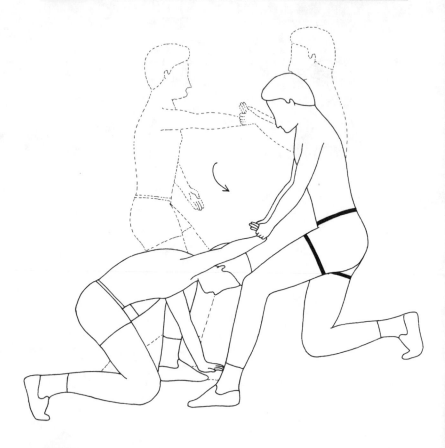

FIGURE 118

FIGURE 119

Figures 119 through 121

Figure 119. The right hand of the opponent is rotated toward the outside of the body, fingers pointed up. This is the normal limit of rotation for the hand. Any further movement in this direction will compress the bones of the wrist.

Figure 120. When the hand is rotated to ten o'clock, the body begins to follow the rotation. The pressure

FIGURE 120

against the wrist would cause a considerable amount of pain at this point.

Figure 121. When the wrist is rotated to seven o'clock, the opponent will either willingly or unwillingly throw his body into the direction of the turn in an attempt to compensate for the twist and alleviate the pressure on the wrist.

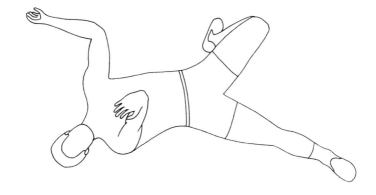

FIGURE 121

FIGURE 122

Figures 122 through 126

Figure 122. Rotating the wrist to the inside of the body will cause similar reactions, but the stroke will be longer and involve more joints, movement, and pressure.

Figure 123. At this point in the rotation, there is no compression of the carpal bones.

Figure 124. At the nine o'clock position, the arm has rotated, and the wrist is thus at its maximum rotation.

FIGURE 123

Figure 125. When the hand is forced up to twelve o'clock, the body begins compensating for the rotation and turns to relieve the pressure.

Figure 126. Forcing the hand to the three o'clock position will cause the opponent's body to compensate further, sending its mass into the air. Using the wrist as a lever allows you to manipulate the entire body.

FIGURE 124

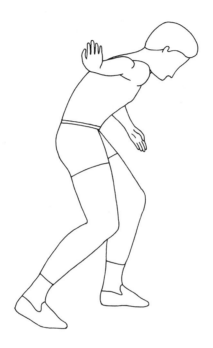

FIGURE 125

FIGURE 126

The Elbow   .

Attacks on the elbow will require a direction of force and a block or opposing force to accomplish the needed leverage for a submission, takedown, or breaking technique. You will recall the analysis of this target in Chapter 3. We will now apply those principles in technical combat.

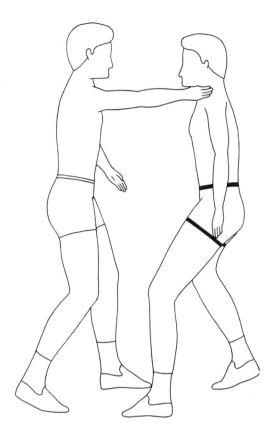

FIGURE 127

Figures 127 through 132

Figures 127 and 128. Starting from the one-hand choke position, bring your extended right arm inside your opponent's right arm and swing up and out in a wide counterclockwise rotation.

Figure 129. As your arm makes contact with your opponent's, tilt your head back to clear the path of his hand as it leaves your neck. By continuing the rotation of your arm, you

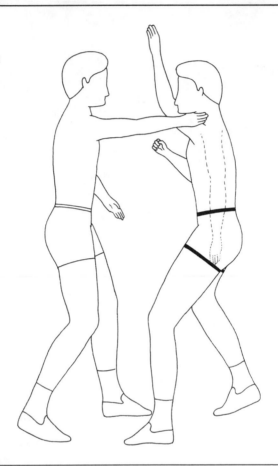

FIGURE 128

force your opponent's hand off your neck. Continue the rotation until reaching the point depicted in this illustration.

Figure 130. As your arm crosses to the outside of your
opponent's arm, bring your elbow to your ribs, trapping
his hand under your arm. Clasp his arm with your hand so
that the heel of your hand is touching the underside of
his elbow joint. Simultaneously deliver a short right half-
turn punch to his chin.

FIGURE 129

Figure 131. From the extension of the punch, bring your right hand under his arm and place the palm over the back of your left hand for a power drive against the elbow.

Figure 132. With a quick, snapping thrust, drive the elbow upward as depicted by the arrow. The joint will hyperextend, damaging the articulating ligaments.

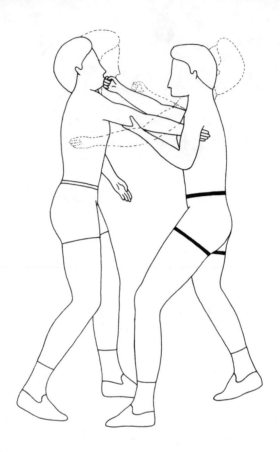

FIGURE 130

FIGURE 131

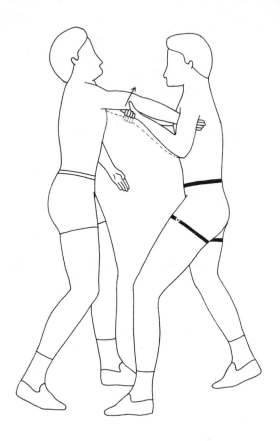

FIGURE 132

FIGURE 133

Figures 133 through 137

Figures 133 and 134. In Figure 133, you are squared off with your opponent. In Figure 134, he has advanced with a right-handed punch to your face. You have caught the incoming punch with a left inside shuto block.

Figure 135. Rotate the blocking palm to the outside, grappling your opponent's wrist. As you make this

FIGURE 134

rotation, extend a half-turn punch with your right hand
to his chin.

Figures 136 and 137. From the punch position, rotate
your right arm upward in a wide circle, coming up under
the opponent's clasped arm, and jam your lower forearm
into the opponent's elbow, driving upward while pulling
down on his wrist with your left hand.

FIGURE 135

FIGURE 136

FIGURE 137

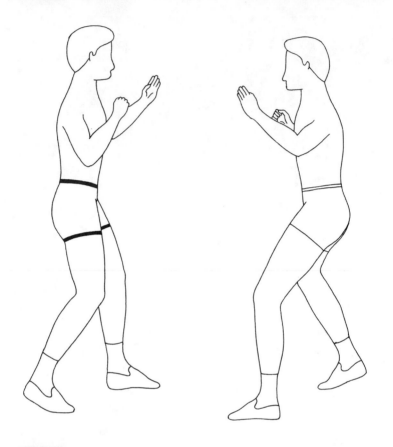

FIGURE 138

Figures 138 through 141

Figures 138 and 139. Again starting from a frontal squared position, your opponent advances with a wide right-hand punch to your face.

Figure 140. Rotate the palm of your blocking hand and grapple the opponent's wrist tightly. As you clasp the wrist, chamber your left foot for a high front kick.

Figure 141. While pulling down on the opponent's

FIGURE 139

wrist, drive a front kick up into the bottom side of his elbow.

FIGURE 140

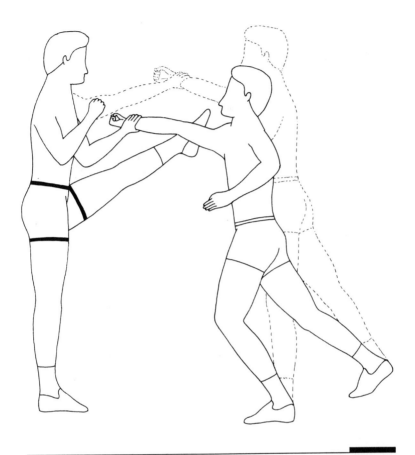

FIGURE 141

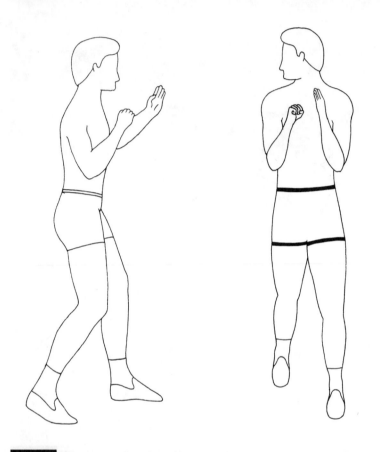

FIGURE 142

Figures 142 through 146

Figures 142 and 143. In this sequence you will be defending yourself from a face punch initiated from your right side. In Figure 143, you block the incoming punch with an inside shuto block and rotate your upper body slightly to the right.

Figure 144. Again, clamp the opponent's right wrist by turning your blocking hand outward and tak-

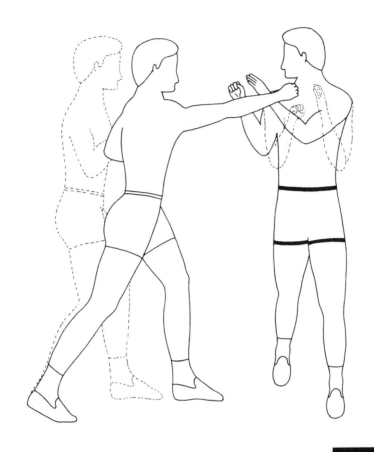

FIGURE 143

ing a tight grip on his arm at the wrist area. Extend a right half-turn punch into his face as you take your grip.

Figure 145. Turn his wrist to the palm-up position and draw back your right arm, held rigid for an upward thrust.

Figure 146. Jam your right arm upward into your opponent's elbow while jerking down on his wrist.

FIGURE 144

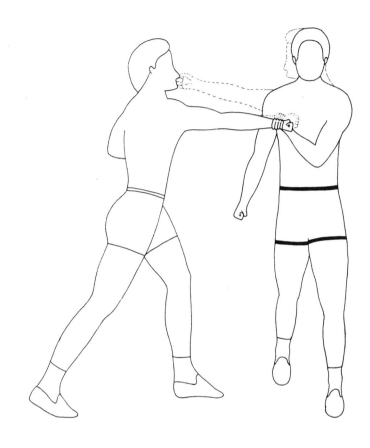

FIGURE 145

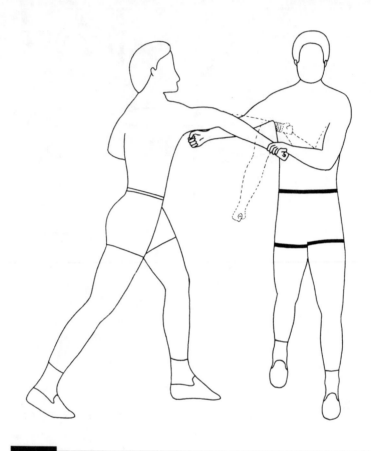

FIGURE 146

CHAPTER SIX

The Cervical Vertebrae

I n the following pages, the final superior transverse plane target, the cervical vertebrae, will be used in technical applications. It is important to re-emphasize that attacks to this area can and most often will be fatal if strength and speed are incorporated into the movements.

To achieve any reasonable level of efficiency in martial arts training, constant, hands-on practice is necessary. You must develop a feel for your own strength, reach, flexibility, and speed. All of the techniques in this book are dangerous to practice, and the potentially lethal target being discussed in this final chapter must be approached with the greatest of care.

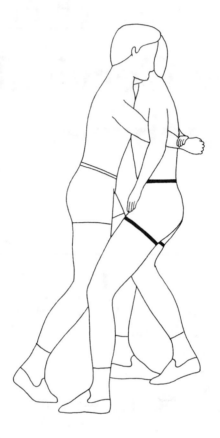

FIGURE 147

Figures 147 through 150

Figures 147 and 148. In Figure 147, your opponent has grabbed you from the front, under the arms. In Figure 148, tilt your head back, reach up with your left hand and take a handful of your opponent's hair firmly in your hand, and place your palm on his chin with the heel of your hand settled to push his head upward to the right.

Figures 149 and 150. Pull down with your left hand

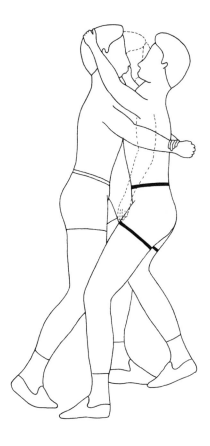

FIGURE 148

while pushing up with your right. This is a high-speed snap movement. Figure 150 illustrates the lines of drive from a facing view.

This technique may be applied while slowly increasing pressure to pry the opponent away from you.

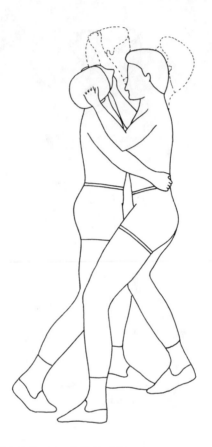

FIGURE 149

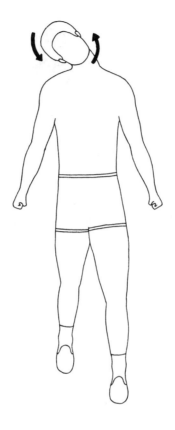

FIGURE 150

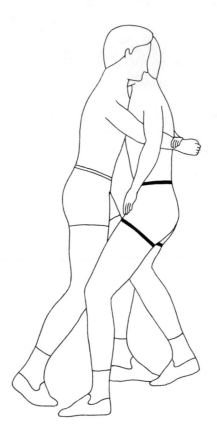

FIGURE 151

Figures 151 through 154

Figures 151 and 152. You are starting again from a front bear hug position. Note the adjustment in the right-hand grip illustrated in Figure 152, as opposed to the grip in Figure 148. We're going to be taking the head in a different direction this time. The grip on the hair is the same.

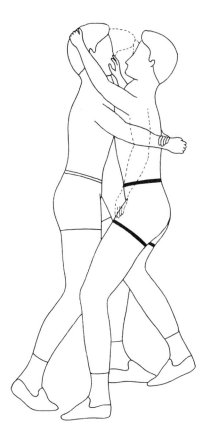

FIGURE 152

Figure 153. Pull straight down with the left hand and drive the chin upward with the right.

Figure 154. Continue the lines of drive with both hands, and the opponent will remain upright but drop right in front of you.

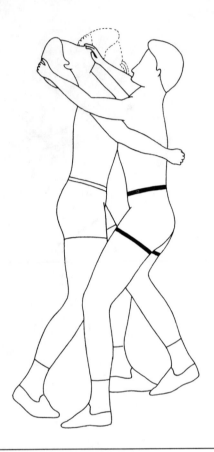

FIGURE 153

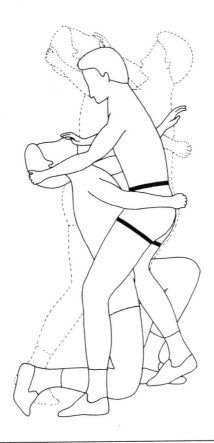

FIGURE 154

FIGURE 155

Figures 155 through 160

Figure 155. This time we will begin from a frontal, squared-off position and use a blocking technique to close the gap between you and your opponent.

Figure 156. Your opponent has advanced with his left foot and has initiated a right-hand punch.

Figure 157. Using a left-handed crossing palm block, guide the extending punch to your right side.

FIGURE 156

Figure 158. As the punch clears your face, palm the offending hand down to the outside of your right hip. Shuffle forward with a short left then right step, and extend a right half-turn punch into your opponent's chin.

Figure 159. From the punch position, lean forward and reach behind your opponent's head. Grab onto a handful of his hair in your right hand.

Figure 160. With a hard, snapping drive, jerk down

FIGURE 157

and back on your opponent's head while stepping back
and dropping to one knee. Properly executed, this movement will turn your opponent over backwards in the air.

FIGURE 158

FIGURE 159

FIGURE 160

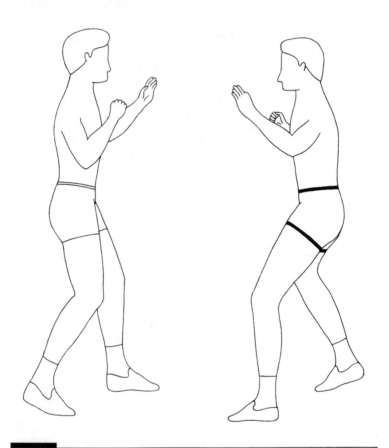

FIGURE 161

Figures 161 through 165

Figures 161 and 162. In this final technique we are again starting from a facing, squared-off position. The advance in Figure 162 is with a low-level punch.

Figure 163. Take a slightly outward, forward step with your left foot and use a low, sweeping palm block to deflect the punch.

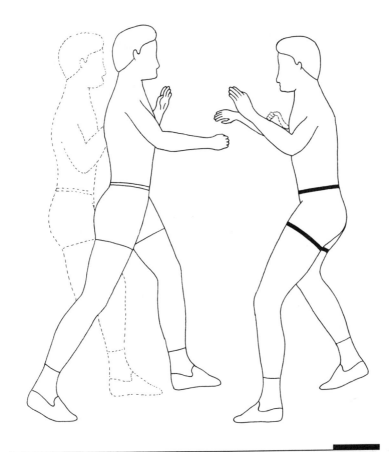

FIGURE 162

Figure 164. Straighten up and take a chin/hair lever grip on your opponent's head.

Figure 165. Although your stroke here is primarily horizontal, it has a slight angle. With a hard-driving snap, push your opponent's chin toward his left shoulder while pulling his hair toward his right shoulder.

FIGURE 163

FIGURE 164

FIGURE 165